Dangerous Animals

Einstein Sisters

KidsWorld

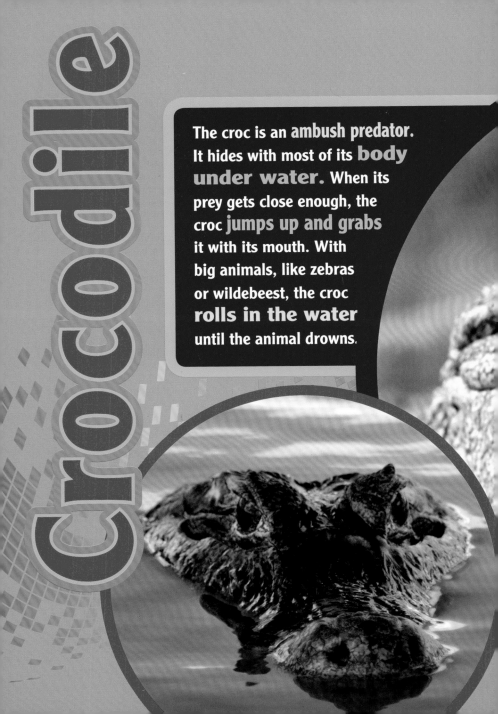

crocodile

The croc is an **ambush predator.** It hides with most of its **body under water.** When its prey gets close enough, the croc **jumps up and grabs** it with its mouth. With big animals, like zebras or wildebeest, the croc **rolls in the water** until the animal drowns.

Poison Dart Frog

It is only about the size of a **toonie,** but the golden poison dart frog has enough toxin to **kill 10 men.** The **toxin** is on the frog's skin. Anything that **licks or touches** the frog gets poisoned.

There are more than 175 different kinds of **poison dart frogs.** Depending on the species, they can be **green, red, blue, yellow** or even **black.**

These **little frogs** live in the **rainforests** of South America. They are some of the **most poisonous** animals in the world.

Hippopotamus

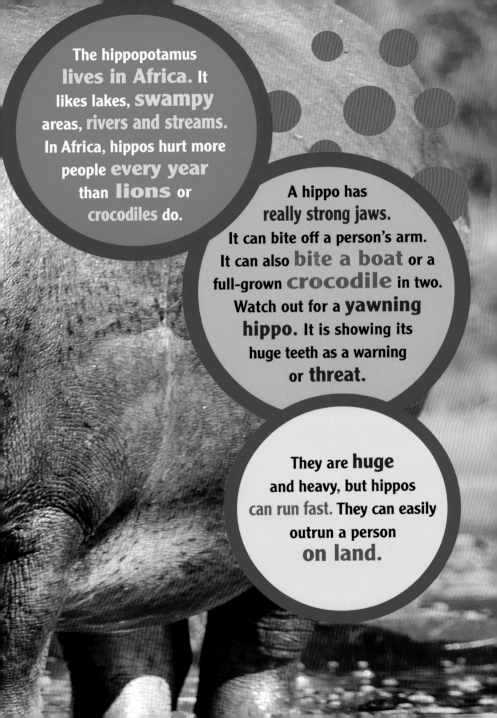

The hippopotamus **lives in Africa.** It likes lakes, **swampy** areas, **rivers and streams.** In Africa, hippos hurt more people **every year** than **lions** or crocodiles do.

A hippo has really strong jaws. It can bite off a person's arm. It can also **bite a boat** or a full-grown **crocodile** in two. Watch out for a **yawning hippo.** It is showing its huge teeth as a warning or **threat.**

They are **huge** and heavy, but hippos **can run fast.** They can easily outrun a person **on land.**

Stonefish

Stonefish usually **live in shallow water.** In Australia, stonefish can stay out of the water for 24 hours. They **lay on the beach** until the next tide comes in.

Box jellyfish live in the ocean around Australia. They are one of the most poisonous animals in the world. Their **toxin** makes a heart stop beating.

They are also called sea wasps.

Box Jellyfish

These jellyfish are pale blue. **Their body,** called a medusa, **is shaped like a box. They can have up to** 60 tentacles **that grow to be almost as long as a** mini van.

They have **24 eyes**, 6 on each side of their body. Most jellyfish just **float in the water**, but box jellyfish actually swim.

Komodo
Dragon

Komodo dragon **saliva is toxic.** It poisons the blood of any animal the **lizard bites,** except other **komodo dragons.** Komodo dragons don't seem to be bothered by the **toxins** in **each other's saliva.**

Most predators eat only the **meat** of their prey. Komodo dragons also eat the **bones** and **even hooves.**

Komodo dragons are the biggest lizards in the world. They **live on islands in Indonesia.**

Young **komodo dragons** spend a lot of time **in trees.** If they stay on the ground, a full-grown **komodo** might eat them. Young komodos will also **roll in poo** so adult komodos won't **eat them.**

Blue-ringed Octopus

The **blue-ringed octopus** is one of the world's **most poisonous** animals. Its toxin can **kill** a person in just **a few minutes**. One octopus has enough poison to kill **10 men**.

This octopus is about the size of a golf ball. It has a grey body, but when it is scared, it has blue rings.

It has no skeleton, so it can squeeze into tiny spaces. This makes it hard to see. Blue-rings have been found in pop bottles and sea shells.

Octopuses have 3 hearts.

It lives in the waters off Australia. It likes shallow water and tide pools, the same places people go to swim.

Great White Shark

Nothing can hide from a great white. The shark has a **special sense** that lets it feel the **electric field** caused by a **heartbeat**.

Great white sharks are one of the three kinds of sharks that attack humans the most often.

Young sharks eat squid, rays, fish and smaller sharks. Adult great whites eat seals, sea lions, dolphins and small whales. Most attacks on humans are "sample bites." The sharks are just curious.

These sharks have a great sense of smell. They can smell one drop of blood in a bathtub filled with water.

Great whites have rows of teeth. When one tooth falls out, another replaces it. Their teeth are shaped like triangles.

Lion

You can tell a lot about a male lion from **its mane**. A long, **dark mane** means the lion is **healthy**.

Lions live in packs called **prides**. **Female lions** do the hunting, and **males** protect the pride.

There are **two types** of lions: African lions and **Asiatic lions**. Asiatic lions live in India. There are **less than 500** Asiatic lions left in the wild.

Lions love to **sleep**. They can sleep for **20 hours a day**.

Lions will eat
almost anything. They
work together to catch **large
animals** like zebras, wildebeest
and **Cape buffalo**. They also
sometimes attack **cattle,
sheep** and **people**.

Black

You can't outrun a black mamba. It is the fastest snake in Africa, and one of the fastest in the world. It can slither as fast or faster than most people can run.

This snake can grow to be as long as a car.

Mamba

Black mambas have the most **poisonous venom** of all snakes. Only 2 drops can **kill a person**. The person can die in less than **20 minutes** if they don't get help.

This snake is very shy. It usually tries to **slither** away from things that scare it. If it can't get away, **it will bite.**

The black mamba **lives in Africa.** It has a brownish grey body. It is called **the black mamba** because the inside of its **mouth is black,** and that's what people see most when **the snake strikes.**

Brazilian Wandering Spider

When this spider is scared, it raises its two front legs over its head and leans back to show off its fangs.

The Brazilian wandering spider is **world's most poisonous spider.** Its poison causes breathing problems and is strong enough to kill a person.

This spider does not build a nest or a web. It **prowls** around the jungle looking for something to eat.

It is active at night and hides during the day. Some of its favourite hiding places are in banana plants and termite mounds. It also hides in people's clothes and shoes.

This spider is **huge!** It is bigger than a dinner plate!

Cassowary

The cassowary lives in the rainforest of Australia and New Guinea. It grows about as tall as a man. It has three toes on each foot. The inside toe has a huge curved claw, and the other two have shorter, straight claws.

It is a shy bird but will attack if it is scared. When it attacks, it jumps in the air and slashes its target with its curved toe. It can also kill an animal with its strong kick.

The cassowary can jump higher than it is tall. It cannot fly but is a fast runner. It has been known to chase dogs, people and even cars that scared it.

The cassowary eats fruit. There is a species of tree in Australia that grows better once a cassowary eats and poos out the seeds.

Piranha

Some types
of piranhas eat plants,
but others **eat meat.** They take
bites from other fish as they swim past.
They also bite chunks out of people
swimming by. Sometimes they
bite off people's **toes**
or **finger tips.**

Piranhas usually
live in schools of about
20 fish. When there isn't enough
food, **piranhas** can form into much
bigger groups. These **big groups** can
attack and kill big animals. Even people
have been killed by piranhas, but
that **doesn't happen**
very often.

Piranhas are
found in the rivers
of South America. They
have huge, **triangle-shaped**
teeth that close like
scissors.

Sloth Bear

The **sloth bear's** favourite foods are **termites**, ants, other bugs and fruit. It also knocks **bee hives** out of trees to eat the honey. Another name for this bear is the **honey bear.**

Sloth bears **live In India.** In some parts of India, people are more afraid of sloth bears than **tigers or leopards.** The big **cats** will often slink away when **surprised** by a person, but a sloth bear will **often attack.**

This bear has **huge,** curved claws. They are perfect for digging into termite mounds or ant hills. They can also really **hurt a person.**

Bull Shark

Bull sharks head-butt their prey before they bite it. They eat anything they can catch.

These sharks like shallow tropical waters. They can also live in freshwater streams. There is even a group of bull sharks living in Lake Nicaragua. They swim from the ocean upstream and jump up the rapids to get to the lake.

Bull sharks are one of the three types of sharks most likely to attack people. They may be the most dangerous because they live in the same places we like to swim.

Bull sharks like to hunt in cloudy water so nobody can see them coming. They can't see very well, so they smell the water for prey.

Moose have **long, strong legs.** Their **front legs** are longer than their **back legs.**

Moose

Male moose are called **bulls**. They **grow antlers** every spring and shed them **in the fall.**

Moose are herbivores, which means they **eat plants.**

The moose **kills more people** every year **in Canada** than any other animal. If someone gets too close to a moose, it might **charge and kick** or **stomp** on the person. A mother moose is really **dangerous** when **protecting her calf.**

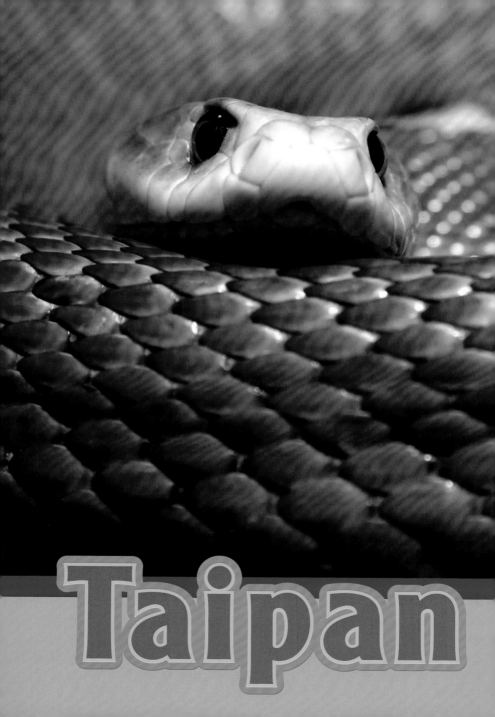

Taipan

The **coastal taipan** is Australia's **most dangerous snake. It** is one of the three most poisonous snakes **in the world.** Its poison paralyzes its prey and makes **it bleed to death.**

There are **three species** of taipan, **the inland, coastal and central ranges taipan. They live in Australia** and **Papua New Guinea.**

Not much is **known** about the **central ranges taipan.**

The inland taipan is also called the **fierce snake.** It lives in the desert. It hides in **cracks** in the ground to get away from the **heat** and **sun.**

The coastal taipan can grow up to **3 metres** long. That's how high a **basketball net** is from the ground. This snake **lives in** forests, **grasslands** and beach dunes. Its **favourite food** is rats.

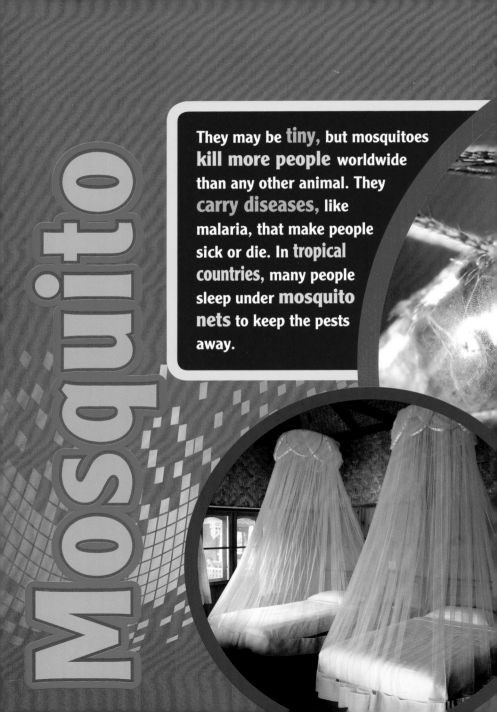

Mosquito

They may be **tiny**, but mosquitoes **kill more people** worldwide than any other animal. They **carry diseases**, like malaria, that make people sick or die. In **tropical countries**, many people sleep under **mosquito nets** to keep the pests away.

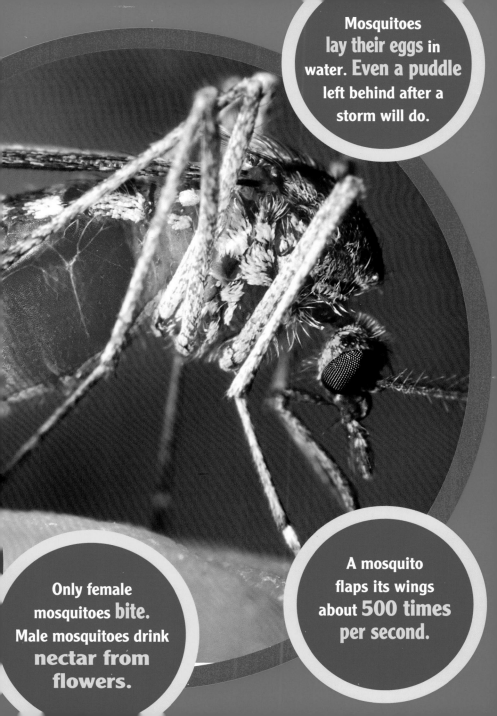

Mosquitoes **lay their eggs** in water. **Even a puddle** left behind after a storm will do.

Only female mosquitoes **bite.** **Male mosquitoes drink** **nectar from** **flowers.**

A mosquito flaps its wings about **500 times** **per second.**

Full-grown **white rhinos** can make 22 kilograms of **poo** per day because they **eat so many plants.** That's 48 times **more** than what a **man** makes.

Rhino

There are **five species** of rhinoceros. White and black rhinos live in Africa. Java, Sumatran and Indian rhinos live in Asia. Indian and Java rhinos have only one horn. The **other rhino species have two.**

All species of rhinos are **endangered.** Poachers kill them for their **horns.** The Java rhino is the rarest. Only about 50 Java rhinos are left in the wild.

Rhinos have bad eyesight. Because they can't really see what is around them, they often charge anything that moves. They are **strong enough to crush a car.**

Leopard seals live in the **cold waters** of Antarctica. Young seals eat krill. **Adult seals eat fish,** squid, penguins and even **other seals.**

They can **leap** out of the water to **grab penguins** off the sea ice.

These seals are **named after the leopard** because they have spots on their coats and because they are **so fierce.** They are also called **sea leopards.**

Leopard seals sometimes **attack** scuba divers. They don't **eat** people, but they can really hurt them. People should **stay out of the water** if leopard seals are **nearby.**

Leopard Seal

Tiger

Tigers are **not picky eaters. They will eat** deer, antelope, pigs, **even bears,** leopards and **elephant calves.** In areas where **tigers live close to people,** they will eat dogs, cows and sometimes people. Most tigers that **attack** people are sick, old or **starving.**

There are not many tigers left in the wild. **People are using a lot of the** land that tigers **need to live** and hunt. When tigers and people **live too close** to each other, it is **dangerous for** everyone.

Puff
Adder

This snake is called a puff adder because it **puffs its body up** before it strikes.

The puff adder is one of **Africa's most dangerous snakes.** It **hurts or kills** more people in Africa than any other snake. A person **can die in 24 hours** if the bite is not treated. Even when treated, some people **lose the arm or leg** that was bitten.

Puff adders can **climb trees.** They are also really **good swimmers.**

The puff adder is a **calm** snake. It does not **threaten or chase** away things that scare it. Instead it stays still, hoping its **camouflage** will keep it safe. This makes it **hard to see.** Many people don't even know it's nearby until they **step on it.**

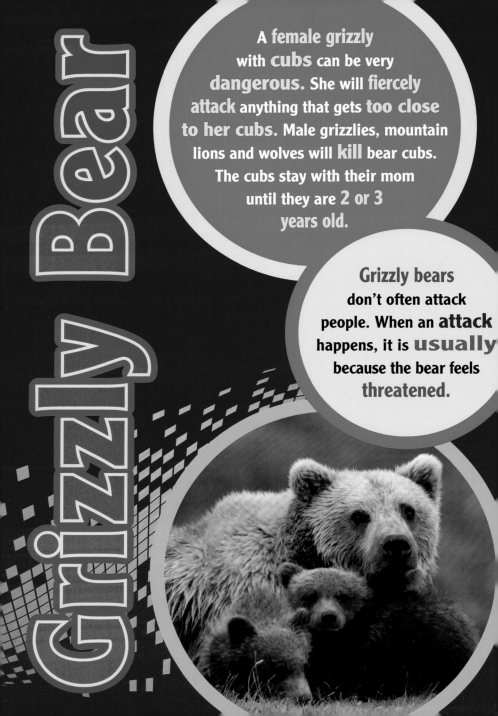

Grizzly Bear

A female grizzly with **cubs** can be very **dangerous**. She will **fiercely** attack anything that gets **too close** to her cubs. Male grizzlies, mountain lions and wolves will **kill** bear cubs. The cubs stay with their mom until they are 2 or 3 years old.

Grizzly bears don't often attack people. When an **attack** happens, it is **usually** because the bear feels **threatened**.

The grizzly bear is one of the **biggest**, strongest animals in North America. The **hump** on its shoulders is made of muscle. Its sharp, **curved claws** are as long as a **human finger**.

Grizzly bears eat plants, berries, nuts, insects, fish, small mammals like **marmots** and sometimes big animals like deer, moose and elk. Female grizzlies are called **sows**. Males are called **boars**.

Australian Funnel-web Spider

Male funnel-webs **bite** more often than females do. They are also **more poisonous** than females.

When the spider **attacks,** it holds onto its victim and bites over and over again. More bites means more **poison** goes into the victim.

Without treatment, people can die from a bite in **less than 20 minutes.**

Australian funnel-web spiders build tunnel- or funnel-shaped webs to catch prey. They like cool, damp places, like under rocks or in wood piles.

These spiders do not go looking for trouble. They only attack people when they feel unsafe.

Orcas do not
see people as food.
No **wild orcas** have ever killed
people. Orcas held in **marine
parks** have hurt or killed
their trainers.

Orcas are
also called **killer
whales,** though they are
actually a **type of
dolphin.**

Orca

They have also been called wolves of the sea because they hunt cooperatively in packs. They will eat anything from a fish or penguin to a blue whale. They can even kill great white sharks.

Orcas live in all the world's oceans. They can be found anywhere from the Arctic to Antarctica.

Orcas have great eyesight. They can see above and below the water. They will often raise their heads out of the water to take a look around.

Fat-tailed Scorpion

Fat-tailed **scorpions** get most of the **water** they need from the **insects** they eat.

Fat-tailed scorpions live in **Africa** and the **Middle East.** They are the **most toxic** scorpions in the world. Their **venom can kill** a man in less than **7 hours.**

They can be **yellow, reddish, brown** or **black.**

Fat-tailed scorpions live in deserts. They are **active at night.** During the day they **hide** in shady places, like **under rocks.** They are sometimes found in **people's houses.**

Scorpions don't bite; they sting. The **stingers** on their tails have a gland that holds **the venom.**

Cape buffalo live in herds of **50 to 500 animals.** If one animal is **attacked,** the herd will help it. The buffalo will **charge their target,** stab it with their horns or stomp on it. They can even kill **lions and hyenas.**

Both males
and females have **horns.**
The males horns are bigger
and **grow together**
into a "boss."

Cape buffalo
eat grass. They can
spend up to **18 hours**
a day grazing.

Cape buffalo
are also called **black
death** or **widowmakers.**
More people are **killed every
year** by Cape buffalo
than by **lions.**

Cape
Buffalo

Leopard

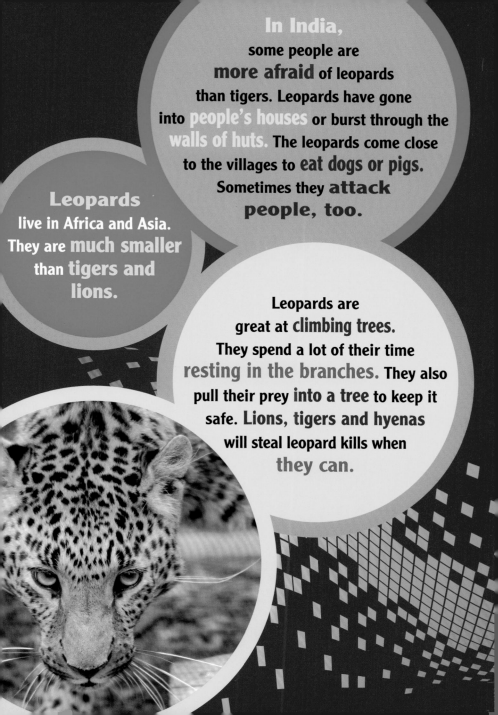

In India, some people are **more afraid** of leopards than tigers. Leopards have gone into **people's houses** or burst through the **walls of huts.** The leopards come close to the villages to **eat dogs or pigs.** Sometimes they **attack people, too.**

Leopards live in Africa and Asia. They are **much smaller** than **tigers and lions.**

Leopards are great at **climbing trees.** They spend a lot of their time **resting in the branches.** They also pull their prey **into a tree** to keep it safe. Lions, tigers and hyenas will steal leopard kills when **they can.**

Tiger
Shark

Tiger sharks are **very curious.** They will **taste anything** they find in the water. Some sharks have **eaten** parts of boats, tires, licence plates, shoes and **jewellery.** They also eat any fish, bird or animal they can catch.

The **tiger shark** is one of the three sharks most likely to **attack people.**

Tiger sharks are named for their stripes. The stripes are **different on every shark.**

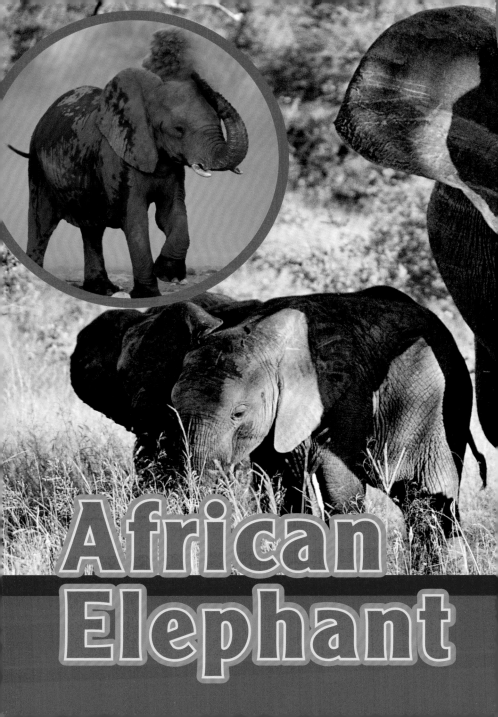

African Elephant

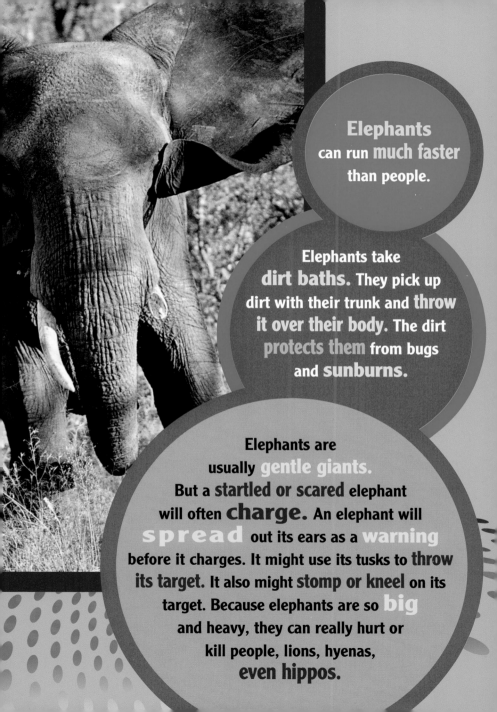

Elephants can run **much faster** than people.

Elephants take **dirt baths.** They pick up dirt with their trunk and **throw it over their body.** The dirt **protects them** from bugs and **sunburns.**

Elephants are usually **gentle giants.** But a **startled or scared** elephant will often **charge.** An elephant will **spread** out its ears as a **warning** before it charges. It might use its tusks to **throw its target.** It also might **stomp or kneel** on its target. Because elephants are so **big** and heavy, they can really hurt or kill people, lions, hyenas, **even hippos.**

The polar bear's **favourite foods** are ringed and bearded seals. It will also eat fish, **walruses**, even stranded whales. Most types of bears are **omnivores**, which means they eat plant foods and meat. Polar bears usually eat only meat.

Polar bears are great swimmers. They can close their nostrils when they dive underwater.

Polar Bear

Polar bears
are a species at risk.
As the Arctic gets warmer,
there is less sea ice. Polar bears
need sea ice to hunt, or they will
starve. They can also drown
trying to swim between ice
floes, if the ice floes
are too far apart.

The Publisher: KidsWorld Books

Library and Archives Canada Cataloguing in Publication

Dangerous animals / Einstein Sisters.

ISBN 978-0-9938401-2-8 (pbk.)

1. Dangerous animals—Juvenile literature. I. Einstein Sisters, author

QL100.D35 2014   j591.6'5   C2014-904201-9

Cover Images: Front cover: Anna Kucherova/Thinkstock. *Back cover:* poison dart frog, Alfredo Maiquez/Thinkstock; hippo, Photowee/Thinkstock; bull shark, Amanda Cotton/Thinkstock. *Background Graphics:* abstract swirl, hakkiarslan/Thinkstock, 7; abstract background, Maryna Borysevych/Thinkstock, 12, 23, 35, 45, 53, 61; pixels, Misko Kordic/Thinkstock, 2, 4, 8, 11, 14, 18, 25, 28, 33, 36, 42, 46, 48, 57. *Photo Credits:* Dennis Donohue/shutterstock, 52–53; Nashepard/shutterstock, 22–23. Thinkstock: 112flieger, 39; Alfredo Maiquez, 4; Amanda Cotton, 30–31, 58–59; Andrea Izzotti, 42–43; Byrdyak, 57; CelsoDiniz, 25; Christopher Meder, 50–51; Craig Dingle, 24; Darren Patterson, 34–35; dirk ercken, 5; Eduard Krslynskyy, 28; eyalcohen, 38–39; filipefrazao, 2; Fuse, 18; ginosphotos, 10; gnagel, 29; Henrik_L, 36–37; Jeanette Zehentmayer, 11; joebelanger, 16–17; Jupiterimages, 3; Koonyongyut, 54–55; LauraDin, 8; mark rigby, 60–61; MikaelEriksson, 9; Mike Schumann, 62–63; MikeLane45, 12–13, 60; milogd, 19; mookandjohn, 20–21; muha04, 6–7; pelooyen, 48–49; PhotosbyAndy, 46; pilipenkoD, 40–41; Purestock, 42; Ron Sanford, 33; sekemas, 32; Simon Bratt, 26–27; singularone, 14; somkcr, 36; StuPorts, 44–45, 56; ViktorCap, 47; Whitepointer, 15; zanskar, 63.

We acknowledge the financial support of the Government of Canada through the Canada Book Fund (CBF) for our publishing activities.

 Canadian   Patrimoine
Heritage   canadien

PC: 27